Century Skills **INNOVATION LIBRARY**

**MAKERS
As Innovators**

Raspberry Pi

by **Charles R. Severance** and
Kristin Fontichiaro

CHERRY LAKE PUBLISHING • ANN ARBOR, MICHIGAN

CHERRY LAKE Publishing

A Note to Adults: Please review the instructions for the activities in this book before allowing children to do them. Be sure to help them with any activities you do not think they can safely complete on their own.

A Note to Kids: Be sure to ask an adult for help with the activities when you need it. Always put your safety first!

Published in the United States of America by Cherry Lake Publishing
Ann Arbor, Michigan
www.cherrylakepublishing.com

Series Editor: Kristin Fontichiaro
Photo Credits: Cover and page 1, ©ZUMA Press, Inc./Alamy; page 5, StuartBrady/commons.wikimedia.org; page 9, ©Maiakat/www.flickr.com/ CC-BY-SA-2.0; page 11, image by Paul Beech, courtesy of the Raspberry Pi Foundation; pages 14 and 18, courtesy of Michigan Makers; page 15, ©mac morrison/www.flickr.com/CC-BY-2.0; pages 21, 27, and 29, ©Nottinghack/www.flickr.com/CC-BY-SA-2.0; page 22, ©whiteafrican/ www.flickr.com/CC-BY-2.0

Library of Congress Cataloging-in-Publication Data
Severance, Charles R.
  Raspberry Pi/by Charles R. Severance and Kristin Fontichiaro.
    pages cm.—(Makers as innovators) (Innovation library)
  Includes bibliographical references and index.
  ISBN 978-1-62431-139-0 (lib. bdg.)—ISBN 978-1-62431-205-2 (e-book)—
ISBN 978-1-62431-271-7 (pbk.)
  1. Raspberry Pi (Computer)—Juvenile literature. 2. Microcomputers—Juvenile literature. 3. Python (Computer program language)—Juvenile literature.
I. Fontichiaro, Kristin. II. Title.
  QA76.8.R15S48 2014
  005.13'3—dc23   2013004929

Cherry Lake Publishing would like to acknowledge the work of The Partnership for 21st Century Skills. Please visit www.p21.org for more information.

Printed in the United States of America
Corporate Graphics Inc.
July 2013
CLFA13

21st Century Skills INNOVATION LIBRARY

Contents

Chapter 1

Making Pi

Most of us spend at least part of each day using a computer, tablet, or smartphone. These devices are designed to be as easy as possible to use. We rarely have reason to peek inside to see how the computer works. A Raspberry Pi computer is different. You can see everything—the **soldering**, the **ports**, and the **circuit board**. Why would someone make a computer and show you the guts? Why would people work six years and donate their own money to create a computer and then charge just $25 to $35 for it? And why did the initial batch of 10,000 Raspberry Pis (nicknamed RasPi) sell out in less than 24 hours?

The story begins in 2006 at England's University of Cambridge Computer Laboratory. A group of people at Cambridge, including Eben Upton, Jack Lang, Rob Mullins, and Alan Mycroft, started noticing that something had changed. When many of them had applied to college in the 1990s, competition to get into a computer science program was fierce. Everybody seemed to come to college already knowing how

The BBC Micro was once a popular computer among beginning programmers.

to program in at least one **language**. Students had often learned programming languages as a hobby on machines like the BBC Micro, the Apple II, or the Commodore 64.

But by the time Upton and his friends had become the teachers, far fewer students came to computer science school with programming experience. This batch of incoming students might have built Web sites or used basic everyday programs, but many did not know how to create their own **software**. This meant that the computer science professors had a harder time finding great incoming students. They spent more college hours teaching skills that students used to have already when they arrived.

Why was that? Maybe it was because computers had gotten a lot easier to use. Maybe it was because there were so many great programs out there that people bought programs instead of writing their own. Maybe kids were spending more time playing video games instead of making them. But for Upton and his friends, writing programs was more fun and more useful. How could they get more people interested in programming?

They thought it would be great if someone could create a really simple, inexpensive, powerful computer that kids could play with and program. That way, parents wouldn't worry about their kids accidentally messing up the family computer.

Most computer companies aren't in the business of making really simple, cheap computers. They would rather make expensive computers so they can make more money. So the teammates decided they'd recruit a few experts and build one themselves. They added Pete Lomas and David Braben to their team. They registered as a not-for-profit organization and called themselves the Raspberry Pi Foundation. Pi is both a joke (pi is a number used in many mathematical formulas that is equal to about 3.14) and a reference to a programming language called Python. And Raspberry? Well, what else goes with pie?

Over the next several years, the teammates worked at other jobs while working to create the new computer in their free time. They asked lots of questions. Should the computer be able to connect to the Internet? How many USB ports should it have to connect other components? What should the RasPi use for a monitor? Could people reuse an old TV or would they need a new monitor? Where would people save their files? Over and over, they reminded themselves that they wanted a computer that was powerful, small, and, above all, cheap.

By spring 2012, the team had raised some money selling stickers with the RasPi logo on them. They had also spent thousands of dollars of their own money.

They had a finished design and just enough money to manufacture 10,000 computers. In March 2012, the team finally released the initial batch of 10,000 units. The computers sold out in one day! Factories quickly went back into production.

Many RasPi owners started tinkering. They wanted to figure out what they could do with a RasPi besides use it to learn to program. Every day, there was a steady stream of new Web pages, videos, photos, and tutorials popping up online. Some excited volunteers started a Web magazine called *The MagPi*. The world was getting very hungry for Raspberry Pi.

How Did People Celebrate The Raspberry Pi Launch?

People were excited to receive their RasPis. Many people posted unboxing videos, which are recordings of them opening the packages. They were surprised that the computers were small and lightweight enough to be shipped in a small padded envelope! Other people added their locations to an online map, showing where in the world the original RasPis were.

Chapter 2

Setting Up

I f you're reading this book, then you are the kind of person that the Raspberry Pi Foundation was thinking about when it created its new computer. Maybe you have a Raspberry Pi at school or home. Maybe you're just curious about programming. In this chapter, we'll take a look at how to set up a Raspberry Pi.

The Raspberry Pi does not come with a case or any accessories.

When you buy a tablet or desktop computer, all the parts you need come in the box. When you buy a Raspberry Pi, your $35 gets you just the RasPi itself. You will need some additional equipment to get started. You might have these already. If not, you can purchase a kit with the additional items that you will need.

Here is what you will get in a typical kit:

- a Model B Raspberry Pi
- an Ethernet cable (to connect your RasPi to the Internet)
- a 4GB SDHC memory card, often found in cameras (to store the **operating system** and programs)
- a micro USB power supply and cable (to provide power to your RasPi)
- a case (to protect your RasPi from dust)

You will also need a screen. You can use an older television with a video input (yellow plug) or a newer television with an HDMI input. You will need a matching cable to connect the Raspberry Pi to your television. You need only one of these two video connections. If you have a choice, you should use an HDMI-capable television. Its images will look much crisper.

RASPBERRY PI MODEL B

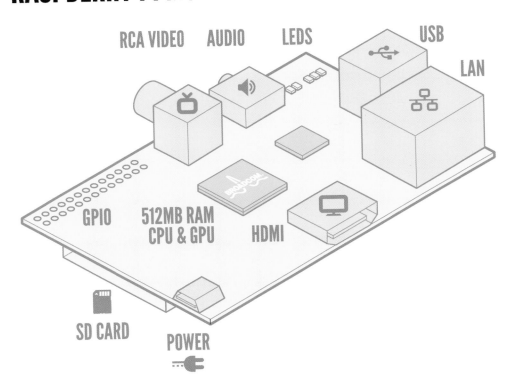

RCA VIDEO AUDIO LEDS USB LAN

GPIO 512MB RAM CPU & GPU HDMI

SD CARD POWER

You'll need to make yourself familiar with the different parts of the Raspberry Pi.

Finally, you will need a keyboard and mouse with USB connections. You may be able to recycle these from an old desktop computer. You can also purchase them.

Before inserting the SD card into the Raspberry Pi, you must install software onto the card using another computer that is running and connected to the Internet.

Plugging In Your Pi

Plugging cables into the Raspberry Pi is very simple. The cables each have different shapes and can be plugged in only one way. The Raspberry Pi is pretty tough, but it is best to hold it by the edges. Each cable should go in easily. You should never have to push very hard. If you have to push hard to insert a cable, something is wrong. Start by plugging in all of the cables except for the USB power cable.

Chapter 3

Installing Linux

All computing devices have an operating system. An operating system is a kind of master brain that tells all the parts—keyboard, mouse, software, and screen—how to work together. The most popular laptop and desktop operating systems are Apple's Mac OS and Microsoft's Windows. Apple and Microsoft make money by building, improving, and selling their operating systems. The next most popular operating system, Linux, isn't owned or sold by anyone. It is open source. This means it is built, modified, and shared for free with anyone. You can download it and use it for free.

The Raspberry Pi was designed for Linux, which needs to be installed on an SD memory card. The SD card functions as the memory for the Raspberry Pi. It will contain your operating system and all your user files. You can switch SD cards when the Raspberry Pi is unplugged. When you turn it on again, the Raspberry Pi will run from the new card. Many students can share one or a few Raspberry Pi computers if each student

Your Raspberry Pi should look something like this once everything is plugged in.

has his or her own SD card that contains an operating system and personal information.

At *raspberrypi.org*, there are instructions for many different ways to install the operating system onto the SD card so the Raspberry Pi can **boot** up. This chapter explains just one of these ways. You do not have to use this particular approach, but one way or another you will need to install Linux on your SD card.

Sometimes installing the operating system on your SD card can be tricky. Be patient and be willing to

Why Do Computers "Boot Up"?

If you connect the Raspberry Pi to a video monitor and turn it on without an SD card, the display will be completely blank. To do anything, the RasPi needs to load software from an SD card. The first software load is called bootstrapping, or booting up. The name comes from the saying "pulling yourself up by your own bootstraps," which means taking care of yourself.

ask people for help. Consider it a challenge, not a problem. Your goal is for this step to be part of the fun of being a RasPi owner. You will learn about using networks and SD cards, finding information on the Web, and other skills. Once you have figured the steps out, you can become a mentor and help others get through the process of setting up their SD cards.

We will take you through the steps of installing the operating system using a free program called

BerryBoot. It is available at *www.berryterminal.com /doku.php/berryboot*. If you have a wired Internet connection, BerryBoot is a simple way to get your Raspberry Pi up and running. If you don't have a wired Internet connection, you may need to use another method to install your operating system. The Raspberry Pi cannot receive wireless Internet signals without an additional wireless adaptor.

The first step is to download the BerryBoot ZIP file from the Web site and double-click it to extract the files into a folder. You can do this on a Windows, Macintosh, or Linux computer. Once you extract the files, you will see about 15 files in the folder. They will have names like berryboot.img and config.txt. Copy all these files onto an empty SD card using an SD card reader. Your computer may have an SD reader built in, or you can connect a separate card reader to your computer using a USB cable.

Once you have copied the BerryBoot files onto the SD card, you can eject the card from your desktop or laptop computer and plug it into the bottom of your Raspberry Pi.

Now you're ready to turn on your RasPi! Unlike other computers, there is no on/off switch. When you plug in the USB power supply, your machine is on. When you unplug it, your machine is off. Turn on your Raspberry Pi and your television or computer monitor.

With your SD card plugged in, your Raspberry Pi now has just enough files to boot up. The files you installed will also tell your RasPi to go online and get all the other files you need to finish installing your operating system.

Within a few seconds of plugging in the Raspberry Pi, you should see a multicolored screen. If nothing appears, check your video connections and make sure your TV is set for the proper input. Shortly after you see the multicolored screen, you should see the BerryBoot setup screen. More detailed instructions

Video Helper

Sometimes it's easier to try something new when you can watch someone else do it first. Before you power up your Raspberry Pi, you might want to watch a video we made that walks you through the entire process. That way, you will have an idea about what will happen as you prepare your RasPi. Check it out at *http://bit.ly /berryboot-pi*.

Be patient as your Raspberry Pi's operating system is installing.

are available at *www.berryterminal.com/doku.php /berryboot*. Carefully read and answer the prompts on the next two screens. Then press OK to continue.

Wait for a few seconds. If your wired Internet connection is working, you should see a list of operating systems including one called Debian

Wheezy Raspbian. That is the version of Linux custom-built and recommended for beginning Raspberry Pi users. Select it, and press OK to start downloading the rest of the operating system.

Downloading the operating system will take a few minutes, but you should see an on-screen display that will show it making progress. Be patient. The download could take 30 to 45 minutes to finish. A small light (known as a light-emitting diode, or LED) labeled LNK on your RasPi will blink as a signal that it is downloading from the Internet.

Once BerryBoot has downloaded and installed the operating system, you will see the BerryBoot menu editor with the newly installed operating system in the on-screen list.

Press Exit, and the Raspberry Pi will reboot and start to load and setup Linux. A series of messages scroll on the screen as Linux is coming up.

These messages might look confusing at first, but they will make more sense as you learn more about the Raspberry Pi. An operating system is a complex piece of software. It takes a number of steps to get it up and running. Windows, Mac OS, and smartphones go through a similar start-up process, but they do not show all the details as they boot up. The Raspberry Pi shows you everything it is doing.

After a minute or two you will see a full-screen text menu that will allow you to customize some features of your operating system.

This box will come up just once. Use the arrows on your keyboard to scroll down to boot_behavior, and then press the Enter key.

Make sure that you select "yes" so that your Raspberry Pi goes straight into the desktop when it boots up. Then use your cursor keys to move to Finish, and press Enter again. When the system asks if you want to reboot, say yes. The Raspberry Pi will then reboot one more time.

This time, after a minute or so, you will see a desktop with a large Raspberry Pi logo and a number of icons. There is a Start menu in the lower right with a Logout option that allows you to shut down the Raspberry Pi before you unplug it.

Congratulations! If you have gotten this far, you have done quite well, learned a lot, and made it past many challenges.

Chapter 4

Writing Your First Program

N ow that you have your Raspberry Pi plugged in and your operating system installed, it's time to start programming. There are many tools

The Raspberry Pi can be programmed to control robotic devices.

preinstalled on your machine and many different Raspberry Pi educational activities available on the Internet. Check out the resources at the back of this book.

History of the Hello World Program

In the program you are about to write, you will be following in the footsteps of many programmers who came before you. Writing Hello World as your first program is a tradition that started at Bell Laboratories (below) in Piscataway, New Jersey, in the 1970s. It showed up in the documents for early programming languages called B and C. B didn't last long, but the C language is still used 40 years later. In fact, the Linux operating system you downloaded is written primarily in C!

While Hello World is a traditional first program, it also emphasizes the nature of what it means to write a program. Even with an operating system fully booted up, the computer still has no idea what to do next. In a sense, it is waiting for you to tell

it what to do. We tell the computer what to do by writing a program. So when we write a program that prints "hello world," it is not the computer saying "hello." Rather, it's a little bit of you inside the computer saying "hello."

You can play games, go online, and learn to program with your Raspberry Pi. In this chapter, we will write a simple Python program. Python is an open-source programming language that many professional programmers use today. Just like some people speak French and some speak Spanish, different computers "speak" different programming languages.

For this exercise, we will write the classic Hello World program. Thousands of programmers like you got started by writing Hello World as their first program.

On your Raspberry Pi desktop, there is an icon labeled IDLE. There is also one labeled IDLE 3. Each of these represents a different version of Python. We're going to use IDLE, which is the classic version of Python. IDLE stands for Integrated DeveLopment Environment. *Integrated* means it allows you to develop, run, test, and **debug** Python programs all with a single tool.

When IDLE starts, it lets you know it is ready for you to type Python commands by giving you a chevron prompt (shaped like this: >>>). At this prompt type: print "hello world". Then press Enter.

IDLE will respond by printing "hello world". In other words, you told IDLE two things: what action to take (print) and the words to print (hello world).

Did it work? Congratulations! You've just joined the community of programmers from around the world.

What if you want to run the program again and again? That means you need to save it. In IDLE, choose File > New Window to bring up a text editor. This will allow you to type your Python program into a text editor and save it to your SD card. You may want to rearrange your windows so you can see everything at once.

Type the following into the text editor: print "Hello world - This is Chuck". (Use your name instead of "Chuck.") From the toolbar, select File and then Save. Name the file hello.py and save it to your desktop. After it saves, select Run and Run Module in the text editor. That will tell your RasPi to show your program's **output** in the Python shell.

Congratulations! You have written a Python program and caused it to execute on your Raspberry Pi. You went into the Raspberry Pi and greeted yourself from inside the computer. Welcome to programming!

Of course, this is just a start. Even if you don't want to be a professional computer scientist, it is a good idea to learn a little bit about programming. The modern world increasingly requires us to use hardware, software, and networks in our daily lives. It is great to have some understanding of how the inside of computer devices work.

Chapter 5

What's Next?

The Raspberry Pi Foundation was surprised to see who their first customers were. They had designed the RasPi for schoolchildren, but many of the first buyers were makers—adults who love playing with technology and seeing what kinds of inventions they can come up with.

The London Zoo announced in Summer 2012 that it was going to use Raspberry Pis for its EyesPi project. Zoo workers planned to connect their cameras to RasPis to help them spot and track wildlife. One man announced that he would put his RasPi in a small boat, use a solar panel to power it, and send the boat across the Atlantic Ocean. Others are thinking of strapping their RasPi and a camera to a drone that can fly quickly into disaster areas and record footage to discover which places need the most help.

Those programmers have spent much more time learning to program than you just did. But if projects like theirs sound like fun, you'll want to keep learning how to write **code**, tinker, prototype, and make things. Find out if your school or library has a makerspace or a programming club you can join. Makerspaces

One maker is designing a boat powered by a Raspberry Pi that he hopes will cross the Atlantic Ocean!

are places where inventors and programmers gather to share ideas and equipment. Some colleges and universities have classes to teach kids how to program and make stuff. Community education organizations, community makerspaces, scouting troops, and robotics clubs are other good spots where you can meet kids who share your interests. If getting places is tough, there are many sites online that can teach you how to program. You'll be writing your own software in no time!

Some users have programmed their Raspberry Pis to play computer games.

Glossary

boot (BOOT) to power up a computer and load the operating system

circuit board (SIR-kit BORD) a thin sheet onto which electrical components are mounted; a Raspberry Pi's circuit board is its green base

code (KODE) instructions written in a programming language that tell a computer what to do

debug (dee-BUHG) to find and fix problems with computer code

language (LAN-gwij) a set of commands that tells a computer how to behave

operating system (AH-puh-ray-ting SIS-tuhm) the software on a computer that supports all of the other programs that run on it

output (OUT-put) the information a computer produces when it runs a program

ports (PORTS) places on computers that are designed for plugging in cables or other devices

software (SAWFT-wair) computer programs

soldering (SAH-dur-ing) joining pieces of metal by putting melted metal in between them and letting it cool

Find Out More

BOOKS

Harbour, Jonathan S. *Video Game Programming for Kids*. Boston: Cengage Learning, 2012.

Upton, Eben, and Gareth Halfacree. *Raspberry Pi User Guide*. Chichester, England: John Wiley & Sons, 2012.

WEB SITES

The MagPi
http://themagpi.com
Read a free monthly magazine about Raspberry Pi hardware and software.

Raspberry Pi Education Manual
http://downloads.raspberrypi.org/Raspberry_Pi_Education_Manual.pdf
Learn more about using your Raspberry Pi.

The Raspberry Pi Foundation
www.raspberrypi.org
Check out the official site of the Raspberry Pi Foundation.

Scratch
http://scratch.mit.edu
Get ideas for how to use Scratch, another free programming software that comes installed with your Raspberry Pi operating system.

Index

About the Authors

Charles R. Severance (left) and Kristin Fontichiaro (right) teach at the University of Michigan School of Information.

RICHMOND HEIGHTS